Inspirational Quotes For Change

Dr. Sarah Thomas

REJOICE
Essential Publishing

Dr. Sarah Thomas/Rejoice Essential Publishing

PO BOX 512

Effingham, SC 29541

www.republishing.org

Unless otherwise indicated, scripture is taken from the King James Version.

Inspirational Quotes For Change/Dr. Sarah Thomas

ISBN-13: 978-1-956775-53-2

Thank you for purchasing this book. Part of the proceeds will go to Across All Boundaries Christian Church's (Columbia, S C) Safe Haven Project: transitional housing for women and children facing life changing challenges.

Dedication

I dedicate this book to the memory of my mother, the late Mother Sallie Mae Thomas, whose unfailing love was the epitome of motherhood. She was my first encounter with the significance of self-expression and wisdom. I also dedicate this book to my resilient, independent, and gifted siblings, who have been supportive of this journey. Finally, I dedicate this project to my nieces and nephews, so they always value learning, knowledge, and wisdom and strive to be the best at whatever they choose to do in life.

Table of Contents

Acknowledgement:

Thanks to my family and friends, who have encouraged me along the way. To all the individuals I have had the opportunity to inspire, be inspired by, or watch their leadership from afar. I want to say thank you for being my inspiration.

Having an idea and turning it into a book can be challenging. The experience is both internally overwhelming and rewarding. I especially want to thank Kimberly Moses of Rejoice Essential Publishing, who helped make this happen. Forever Grateful! Last, but most important, I thank Yahweh for giving me the mercy and grace to fulfill this project. All Glory goes to Him, who is the Creator of all.

Inspirational Quotes For Change

Introduction

Your mindset is everything!

"As a man thinketh in his heart, so is he" -Proverbs 23:7

Your mindset is a magnet. If you think of blessings, you attract blessings. If you think of problems, you attract problems.

Always cultivate good thoughts and always remain positive and optimistic. So many people are battling with their purpose and meaning in life. New perspectives on your ideas can encourage you to keep thinking and growing. Reading a quote is like obtaining a coach. A confidante, mentor, or inspirational quotes are like that voice in your ear, saying, "Come on! You got this!"

Are you asking questions like, "Who Am I? What is my purpose? What is my destiny? A quote can validate what you think you know about yourself. If you see yourself as resilient, quotes about conquering fears or problems will resonate with you.

When you know who you are, whose you are, and how you have been designed by the Most High God, you have been gifted to your "calling". This inspirational quote book is intended to give you that extra push into your destiny.

HOW TO USE THE BOOK?

From a lifelong, devoted Christian and educator passionate about self-development and the Word of God, this book is an easy read. It is designed to be read on a regular basis. The quotes are selected to:

1. help reduce the effect of shame and guilt in your life.
2. help you find peace instead of storms, and
3. help you know that the power of your thinking can help change others around you.

Research shows that positive thinking has a scientific basis, and though you may not be able to change the world, you can change how you perceive it and how you ultimately respond to it. Possessing this attitude can help change the way you feel about yourself and others, which can have an insightful effect on your own well-being.

Quotes

If you want blessings, be one!

You attract people by the qualities you display. You keep them by the qualities you possess.

Your attacks will always indicate and confirm your assignment.

The enemy wouldn't be attacking you if something very valuable wasn't inside. Thieves don't break into empty houses.

Be patient. Sometimes you have to go through the worst to get the best.

Some people will only love you as much as they can use you. Their loyalty ends where the benefits stop.

When we pray, God hears more than we say, answers more than we ask, and gives more than we can imagine.

Don't block your blessings trying to do people how they do you!

Spiritual maturity isn't measured by how high you jump in praise, but by how straight you walk in obedience.

When things are down, look up! Life brings us both good and bad. What matters most is how we deal with it.

When I lost my excuses, I found my results.

Give God your weakness and he will give you His strength.

Prayer is Powerful! But remember that God works in His timing, not yours. Have patience.

You don't need to monitor things you've left in God's hands.

People are waiting for you to slip, but every time you slip, it's into more blessings.

Don't quit. Someone is praying for you. You will make it through this. God is on your side.

Inhale-Exhale-Repeat
Let it go!

You need to align yourself with people who fit your destiny, not your history.

Your value doesn't decrease based on someone's inability to see your worth.

Everything will happen for you all of a sudden and you'll be thankful you didn't give up.

God is opening the windows of heaven and pouring out blessings for you today! Receive it!

God hears you. Keep praying.

When you hold grudges, your hands are not free to catch blessings.

My mother always told me, "If you can't say anything nice, don't say anything at all," and some people wonder why I'm too quiet around them.

Don't ever try to mess up someone's life with a lie when yours can be destroyed with the truth.

Never argue with toxic people. They will drag you down to their level and beat you with experience, in that order.

Stay focused! Trust God's timing and He will open doors no man can shut.

Trust in God no matter how dark your situation is. God says, "You are coming out." Proverbs 3:5-6.

When you say "yes" to others, make sure you are not saying "no" to yourself.

Sometimes the issue is simply that their ceiling is your floor.

Attract what you expect.
Reflect on what you desire.
Become what you respect.
Mirror what you admire.

Never feel guilty for cutting someone off when they handed you the scissors.

Be happy. Not because everything is good, but because you can see the good in everything.

Stop watering things that were never meant to grow in your life.

You are about to become everything they feared you would be. Don't be distracted.

It doesn't matter who is in the White House, as long as God is in your house.

Trust God today, no matter how dark your situation is. You are coming out! Believe that!

When you stop chasing the wrong things, you give the right things a chance to catch up.

Characterize people by their actions and you will never be fooled by their words.

Don't mistake silence for weakness. Smart people don't plan big moves out loud.

A strong woman knows how to keep her life in order. Even with tears in her eyes, she still manages to say, "I'm okay with a smile."

If they want to leave, let them. If they push you away, go.

You weren't put on this earth to convince anyone of your worth.

Difficulties in your life do not come to destroy you, but to help you realize your hidden potential and power.

The anointing that's on your life attracts attacks! Don't look at it as trouble. Look at it as confirmation!

The people in your life should be a source of reducing stress. Not causing more of it.

Satan tries to limit your praying because he knows your praying will limit him.

You can't change what's going on around you until you start changing what's going on within you.

You are about to birth something so BIG! They'll wish they treated you differently.

Sometimes the grass is greener on the other side because it's fake.

Remember, whatever you do behind someone's back, you are also doing in front of God's eyes.

God has a habit of picking nobodies and making them somebodies without consulting anybody.

Far too many people are looking for the right person, instead of trying to be the right person.

Your breakthrough is on the way. God is about to turn some things around in your favor. Trust Him!

Every day is a gift from God. Be thankful!

Take care of yourself first or you will have nothing left to give others. Self-care is not selfishness. You cannot serve from an empty vessel.

When you've already prayed about something, stop worrying about it. God has heard you. His time, not yours. He's got you!

I like when I don't have to be careful what I say. That's when you know you're with the right people.

When your worth isn't based on their claps, you won't be broken by their silence.

If you listen carefully enough, someone will tell you exactly the kind of person they are. Sit back and listen.

Everyone makes mistakes in life, but it doesn't mean they have to pay for them for the rest of their life. Sometimes good people make bad choices. It doesn't mean they are bad. It means they are human.

Stay around people who look more like your future than your past.

You're stepping into a chapter of answered prayers. Watch God!

I'm blessed with everything I need. I am working hard towards everything I want. And most of all, I appreciate and thank God for what I have.

Stay humble and give the Glory to God!

There's a message in the way a person treats you. Just listen.

Give your life to God. He can do more with it than you can.

Don't be jealous of anyone, be inspired. We all get the same twenty four hours to grind.

You have not missed your season and time. God is just getting started! What He starts in your life, He will complete.

Life is so much simpler when you stop explaining yourself to people and just do what works for you.

Don't try to rush God's plan for your life. Everything will happen exactly when it is supposed to happen. Have patience, faith, and never stop believing.

You can't pour from an empty cup. Take care of yourself first.

Don't dull your shine for anybody. The people who need your light are more important than those who don't want you to shine.

Sometimes it's better to just remain silent and smile.

When life gives you more than you can stand, kneel.

When my circle got smaller, my vision got clearer. There's strength in loyalty, not numbers. Pay attention.

Reputation is what you think of me. Character is what God knows of me!

Sometimes you have to let things go, so there's room for better things to come into your life.

Growth is often mistaken for "acting funny."

Your truest friends are the people who don't walk out the door when life gets hard. They actually pour some coffee and pull up a chair.

Be willing to walk alone. Many who started with you won't finish with you.

Everything will work out in the end. You don't need to know how. You just have to trust God and believe that it will.

It is what it is. It was what it was. It will be what it will be. Don't stress about it.

Peace is not the absence of trouble, but the presence of Christ.

As I grow older, I pay less attention to what people say. I just watch what they do.

If you don't heal what hurt you, you'll bleed on people who didn't cut you.

When asked if my cup is half full or half empty, my only response is that I am thankful I have a cup.

The humble have no problem winning in silence because they're not looking for an applause from the crowd.

As we grow older, we don't lose friends. We just learn who the real ones are.

At the end of the day, it's not about those who let you down. It's about those who always held you up.

Spend more time with people who bring out the best in you, not the stress in you.

Don't shine so that others can see you. Shine so that through you, others can see Him.

If you really want them out of your life, then remove yourself.

If you want to soar in life, you must learn to fly (first love yourself).

A lie doesn't become truth, wrong doesn't become right and evil doesn't become good, just because it is accepted by a majority.

When God is elevating you, your company will change.

Friendship is not about who acts true to your face. It's about people who remain true behind your back.

Never lie to someone who trusts you and never trust someone who lies to you.

Be the type of energy that no matter where you go, you always add value to the spaces and lives around you.

People will throw stones at you. Don't throw them back. Collect them and build an empire.

The saddest thing about betrayal is that it never comes from your enemies.

People come and go, but the right ones stay.

Today is a new day. Make the most of it.

Don't measure the size of the mountain. Just talk to the one who can move it.

Fight all of your battles on your knees.

Nothing is permanent. Don't stress yourself too much because no matter how hard the situation is it will change.
God will use you.

God has a plan. Trust it, live it, enjoy it.

Unless you know who you are, you will always be vulnerable to what people say. Do you.

You're never in control of what they give you, but you're always in control of what you accept.

You have entered into a season of answered prayers! When you pray, God shall answer swiftly!

Stay Positive!

The things you're praying and hoping for tend to arrive at the most unexpected moments.

When it's your turn, it doesn't matter if you're at the back of the line. God will move you to the front.

Stop pressing rewind on the things that need to be deleted from your life. Your past doesn't have your healing. Your future does.

Pray.
No matter what problems you're facing, just pray. God is listening.

There will always be someone who can't see your worth. Don't let it be you.

God already turned that situation around. Go ahead and rejoice. It's done!

You can't become who you want to be because you're too attached to who you've been.

People who judge you by your past don't belong in your future.

Quit dismissing folks over what you heard. God hasn't dismissed you over what He knows.

God did it!

As you evolve, you will make a lot of people uncomfortable. Evolve anyway.

God made you the way you are for a reason. Besides, an original is worth more than a copy. Be Yourself.

It's a great day to have a great day! You are blessed inspite of.

Faith tells me that no matter what lies ahead of me, God is already there. Trust God.

No regrets. Just lessons learned.

Ordinary prayers get ordinary results. God meets us at the level of our faith. If you ask small, you will receive small.

The safest place in all the world is in the will of God.

God hears you. Keep praying.

Your prayer request is about to become your praise report! Praise Him in Advance.

Be selective in your battles, for sometimes peace is better than being right.

What if everything you are going through is preparing you for what you asked for?

Stay away from negative people. They have a problem for every solution.

Let go of the people who dull your shine, poison your spirit, and bring you drama. Cancel your subscription to their issues.

Re-set, re-adjust, re-start, re-focus, as many times as you need to.

Almost everything in your life is a reflection of a choice you have made. If you want a different result, make a different choice.

He's God, not "god."

Do everything with a good heart and expect nothing in return. You will never be disappointed.

Find a reason to laugh. It may not add years to your life, but it will add life to your years.

If not now, when?

Turn your worry into worship and watch God turn your battle into blessings. It's a peaceful purpose.

Every closed eye is not sleeping and every open eye is not seeing.

Things are about to happen suddenly! God has been working behind the scenes. Get ready for a rapid shift! Watch God.

Blessed in silence.
Do it God!
Elevation is here.
Watch the shift.

Give so much time to the improvement of yourself that you have no time to criticize others. God is pruning, molding, and searching me. Do it God!

Every time I thought I was being rejected from something good, I was actually being redirected to something better. I'm a God chaser.

Just because you don't see anything happening, doesn't mean God is not working. A strong finish equals strong faith.

God is fighting your battles, arranging things in your favor and making a way even when you don't see a way. Be encouraged.

A glowing woman can help other women glow and still be lit.

No response is a response and it's a powerful one. Remember that.

Some people create their own storms, then get upset when it rains.

If you have a family that loves you, a few good friends, food on your table and a roof over your head. You are richer than you think.

Never allow waiting to become a habit. Live your dreams and take risks. Life is happening now.

Real growth is when you start checking and correcting yourself. Instead of blaming others, take your power back by being responsible for your life.

Don't be afraid of losing people. Be afraid of losing yourself by trying to please everyone around you.

I don't trust words. I trust actions. People can tell you anything, but actions tell you everything.

The gap between the life you want and the life you are living is called mindset, focus, and consistency.

When you settle for crumbs, you will always be starving. Think Big!!

Only what you do for Christ will last!!

The most convincing sign that someone is truly living their best life, is their lack of desire to show the world that they're living their best life. Your best life won't need outside validation.

Don't let old hurts inhibit new beginnings.

They told me I couldn't. That's why I did.

Don't underestimate what God is doing in your season of waiting. Delayed but not denied!!

Change doesn't happen when circumstances improve. A change happens when you decide to improve your circumstances.

Live your life with no regrets!!

When you do something out of love, you do not count the cost.

There will always be someone who doesn't see your worth. Don't let it be you.

You are about to become everything they feared you would be.

A religious person will do what he is told... no matter what is right... whereas a spiritual person will do what is right... no matter what he is told.

Life is Like a Camera: Focus on what is important. Capture the good times. Develop from the negatives. And if things don't work out, just take another shot.

Eventually, you'll realize God was connecting the dots all along. Trust Him.

None of us sit high enough to look down on anybody.

God doesn't give us what we can handle. God helps us handle what we are given.

God is never late.

You'd be surprised who's watching your journey and being inspired by it. Quitting is not an option.

A person's most beautiful asset is not a head full of knowledge, but a heart full of love, an ear ready to listen and a hand willing to help others.

God is still writing your story. Quit trying to steal the pen and trust the Author.

A smart person knows what to say. A wise person knows whether or not to say it.

Live in a such a way that those who know you, but don't know God, will come to know God because they know you.

We don't walk away to teach people a lesson. We walk away because we finally learned ours.

Happiness is not about getting all you want. It's about enjoying all you have.

I am no longer accepting the things I cannot change. I am changing the things I cannot accept.

When you want different for yourself, you have to start moving differently. Old keys don't unlock new doors.

If you want to know someone's mind, listen to their words. If you want to know their heart, watch their actions.

God is more concerned about your character than your coins. Increasing your coins won't increase your character, but increasing your character can increase your coins.

God has already prepared the way. He's just preparing you.

You can't become who you want to be because you're too attached to who you've been.

Perhaps it's when you walk through darkness, that you understand and value the light.

So many people from your past know a version of you that no longer exists anymore. Growth is beautiful. Let your actions reflect the current you.

If you focus on the hurt, you will continue to suffer. If you focus on the lesson, you will continue to grow.

God didn't bring you this far to only bring you this far.

Not every closed door is locked. PUSH!!

Life is not about expecting, hoping, and wishing. It's about doing, being, and becoming.

Inside every person you know, there's a person you don't know.

Sometimes you simply need to press pause. It's ok.

Don't say God has been silent when your bible has been closed.

Don't you dare shrink yourself for someone else's comfort. Do not become small for people who refuse to grow.

Sometimes losing people makes you find yourself.

Sometimes the things that break your heart, end up fixing your vision.

Worry about your character and not your reputation because your character is who you are, and your reputation is only what people think of you.

Don't feel bad for making decisions that upset other people. You're not responsible for their happiness. You're responsible for yours.

You can't give your life more time, so give the time you have left more life.

Friendship isn't about who you've known the longest. It's about who walked into your life, and said, "I'm here for you," and proved it.

Stay quiet about your goals. Soon, your results will do all the talking.

Remember, most of your stress comes from the way you respond. Adjust your attitude, and all that extra stress is gone. No response is a response.

Successful people reject rejection.

Your value doesn't decrease based on someone's inability to see your worth.

A healthy attitude is contagious, but don't wait to catch it from others. Be a carrier.

The only people who are mad at you for speaking the truth are those people who are living a lie. Speak the truth anyway.

Glass ceilings are shattering everywhere lately! So many women have been appointed and promoted to positions where they are the "first". I'm loving every minute!!

The greatest prison people live in is the fear of what others think.

Never make a permanent decision based on a temporary emotion. Remember that!!

<u>ENDING QUOTE</u>

Everybody can be great because anybody can serve.
You don't have to have a college degree to serve....
You only need a heart full of grace. A soul gener-
ated by love. Dr. Martin Luther King, Jr.

About The Author

Dr. Sarah Thomas is an Associate Professor at Columbia International University and brings over thirty years of human services experience. She worked with the South Carolina Mental Health as Director of Children and Family Services. Prior to working with the South Carolina Department of Mental Health, Dr. Thomas was employed with the South Carolina Department of Social Services/Managed Treatment Services as a Program Director for a Public Therapeutic Foster Care Program and a Wrap Services Program.

Dr. Thomas has been named employee of the year both with SC Department of Mental Health and SC Department of Social Services/Managed Treatment Services. She received numerous awards for outstanding service, commitment and significant contributions for the success of programs for children, adolescents and their families in South Carolina.

Dr. Thomas is an educator, inspirational speaker, counselor, mentor, coach, entrepreneur, philanthropist, and an author. She has been a speaker at conferences, workshops, and seminars. Dr. Thomas has worked several years as an Adjunct Professor at S C State University. She worked as an In-Service Staff Trainer at Claflin University. In addition, Dr. Thomas is the founder of Lighthouse of Deliverance Outreach Ministries in Orangeburg, SC.

Dr. Thomas' educational background includes a Bachelor of Science in Therapeutic Recreation from Benedict College, a Master of Science in Individual and Family Development from South Carolina State University, and a Doctor of Philosophy in Human Services from Capella University. She is a certified Human Development Consultant, and a Master Life and Business Coach. She is a member of the National Organization for Human Services, Southern Organization for Human Services, and Alpha Kappa Alpha Sorority, Inc.

www.ingramcontent.com/pod-product-compliance
Lightning Source LLC
Chambersburg PA
CBHW070956120626
46546CB00004B/1640